Leadership

Quickly Boost Your Self-Confidence With These Top 21
Tips That You Can Put Into Action Today to Create an
Empowered You

*(Unleash the tenacity that is inside you, and strengthen
your resilience)*

Damon Wilkerson

TABLE OF CONTENT

Introduction

There are numerous books produced on different aspects of business, such as company culture, business management, organization behavior, organization psychology, employee retention, and so on. However, each of these books focuses on a distinct topic, and it may be challenging to link the many business ideas that are discussed in separate books in an integrated manner. People from all over the world must have read a lot of books in an effort to improve their skills as corporate leaders, yet despite this, the business world seems to be suffering from a shortage of effective leaders. There are effective leaders in the business world, but there are also ineffective leaders in the market. If we hadn't had poor leadership, then none of our businesses would have been doomed when they opened their doors. A review of the corporate market reveals, however, that there have been many unsuccessful leaderships, many unsuccessful commercial organizations, many unsuccessful leaders, and many incorrect judgments made. In order to promote objective business leadership, we came up with the idea of combining those several distributions into a single book. Bruce Lee, a well-known martial artist who formerly lived on our planet, was a proponent of the ideology of unifying several styles of martial arts in an integrated manner, with the goal of selecting the most effective techniques from each. And without a shadow of a doubt, he was an unrivaled victor throughout his whole life. Bruce Lee was a proponent of the idea that there should be an objective manifestation of martial arts, breaking them down into their essential elements. In a similar manner, we have gleaned the fundamental concepts that are required for the operation of a corporate or commercial organization that is sustainable. Additionally, in this day and age of 'the internet of things' and 'artificial intelligence,' objective clarity is necessary for the management of any firm. Our time spent in school has also provided us with a few important life lessons. In the context of today's interconnected world, the subjective method of gaining an understanding of the processes, procedures, and instruments involved in operating a corporation is insufficient. Over the course of fifteen years, we have interacted with a diverse range of workers and employers. We were able to learn valuable lessons from our business contacts and acquaintances who worked in corporations, with whom we had the opportunity to discuss the complexities of management. Additionally, conversations were held with engineering graduates and MBA graduates in order to interrogate their knowledge of corporate architecture and corporate procedures. We saw what's known as a 'conceptual gap' among those kids. In today's day and age, we can see that there is a divide between employees and employers, and neither party is getting along swimmingly. We have gone through the operational aspects of organizational management and development while keeping the objective character of leadership in mind throughout our conversation. Insofar as business operations are concerned, the primary topics covered in this book are macromanagement and the link between that and micromanagement. If company executives, entrepreneurs, and start-up companies want a growth culture that is unrestricted, they should implement the 35 principles that are outlined in this book. Many new businesses are doomed to fail quickly because their founders lack focus and because their operational and managerial procedures are inadequate. We have made an effort to convey business principles in a way that dispels the misunderstandings that are held by the many corporations and organizations. The new businesses would have a better chance of surviving if they read our book. People who work in corporations or who are planning to work in corporations should take on the mindset of a leader in order to develop themselves and perform well within the context of the corporation, which will ultimately promote their own personal development. There are a total of 35 chapters in this book, and each one outlines a different business theory along with a concrete plan of action in the form of a "corporate lesson." Each chapter also provides the psychological perspective in context to corporate observation and implementation, linking the neurological element of human beings in context to corporate psychology, hence providing support for the observation and action module that was subsequently followed. While reading this book, everybody and everyone will be able to link their own professional experiences and perspectives. If 'Concepts of Psychology' are not implemented in a commercial enterprise, it is impossible for such enterprise to operate at its full potential. In addition, the chapters in this book focus on the 'potential impacts' that come with job experience.

The book is notable for being clear and objective throughout, making it easy to comprehend. This is the book's most notable quality. In the same way that we are aware of some things that are required for life, we are also aware of certain business concepts that are required for the continued existence and expansion of a business.

Agriculture was prominent throughout this time period, and it was accorded a significant deal of significance. People were involved, and things progressed. After it, a period marked by the rise of industry as a direct result of technical advances arrived. People began adopting new ways of living as well as professional identities. Then the age of information technology arrived, and that's when we first saw the internet's expansiveness. The time has come, at long last, for the implementation of artificial intelligence, which will see robots working concurrently with humans in a competitive environment. However, regardless of the time period, human people have always been the ones in charge of directing the "development engines." War broke out, and while most things came to a halt, business continued as usual. As a result, we have reached the conclusion that notable human beings come up with procedures and demonstrate leadership qualities in order to govern and manage company. Despite the challenges, business has continued to develop. We are now living in a very competitive corporate environment, and in order for us to make it through, we are in need of objective corporate training. Hope is a book that dispels the readers' uncertainties and guides them into positions of preeminent leadership.

What Exactly Does It Mean To Be Successful?

Many of us use the term "success" casually, but we don't fully understand what it means. Success is one of those topics that often comes up in conversation. It is difficult for us to specify precisely what it is that we need to accomplish and how we need to go forward in order to achieve success because of this. Therefore, to begin this chapter, we are going to take a look at what exactly the concept of success is, as well as how we might work toward achieving it.

It would seem that we all need it. It seems like all of us are looking for it. It seems that "success" has become the catchphrase for what we seek, make preparations for, choose, and desire. It's the way that we typically explain our life to other people. We are often taught that success is measured by one's financial well-being, level of public praise, and level of political influence. In the case that we are unable to get it, we are overcome with feelings of envy for others who are successful. Some people who believe that they have lost the potential to be successful have mental breakdowns, midlife crises, and even become ill from merely pondering the prospect. Others give up and come to the conclusion that success isn't as important as just having a job and ensuring that there is food on the table; they conclude that this is more important than achieving their goals. Some people, at the end of their life, come to the startling realization that they have squandered their opportunities and that the things they believed they had were illusory at best.

The average American has a propensity to judge their level of success based on their level of wealth and the things that money can buy for them. People from all over the world think of us as a very materialistic country, one that is always chasing after things and that measures success by the trinkets that money can buy, such as the cool cars we drive, the size of our houses, and the fashionable clothing we wear. In addition to that, it is only what we get — more goods. This does not imply a higher level of happiness or the ability to contribute in any way to a discernible improvement. In essence, it suggests other things.

To a greater or lesser extent, people in many countries measure their level of success based on whether or not their employment allows them to maintain their family life. If they get satisfaction from their profession, are able to spend quality time with their families as a result of it, and maintain a healthy lifestyle as a result of it, then they will consider themselves to be successful. For example, a question was posed to an Israeli screenwriter about whether or not she had made plans to go to Los Angeles in order to make an application to work in the Hollywood film business. Her response was that she would not since she did not want to be too apart from her family. She said that this was the reason. For her, wealth would be exemplified by the fact that she would be able to produce her film in Israel without sacrificing the time she spends with her family.

A few people have the mindset that adequate performance constitutes accomplishment. The question that has to be answered is: Would they say that things are starting to move forward? Is it true that they are succeeding in reaching their business goals? Do their contributions enhance the overall quality of the work that has to be done? If they are successful, it will mean that the project they are working on improves as a direct result of the help they provide. They are able to see the consequences of their labor and are subsequently pleased by it. In addition, they are aware that their job satisfies others, either as a result of the fact that the product they produce is valued or as a result of the fact that the service they provide is helpful.

Some people judge their level of success based on how well their jobs fit their skills and interests, as well as the amount of enjoyment they get from the fruits of their labor. They define it by the pleasure they have while doing the job, the pleasure they experience after they have finished the task, and the pleasure that others experience as a direct result of the work they have performed. In the event that their job does not contribute to their sense of pleasure and enjoyment of themselves as well as other people, then they do not feel effective no matter how much money they have made or how many accolades they have accepted. This is true regardless of the amount of revenue that they have earned. This enjoyment is a result of the work that they have done on their own as well as the work that they have done together with other competent people who contribute their talents to the endeavor and bring harmony to the working relationship. Discord is not conducive to productive work for anybody. Many individuals find that they are unable to enjoy their job and that they do not have a sense that they are making progress when the relationships they make at work are not pleasant and acceptable.

The only challenge is figuring out what to do next. You are all by yourself at the corporate office where you work; no one is present to assist you. Your tools, which include a computer, a desk, a phone, and the other standard equipment that everyone has, have been provided to you by HR. You stand there, staring at the walls, thinking, "What the hell have I gotten myself into?"

This is perfectly normal, and if you are reading this book, you have either already been through this stage or are now through it. You are the only one who can teach yourself how to be a manager. You are not provided with any instruction since it is presumed that you are already competent. Therefore, individuals put on an act; they attempt to be like the manager they saw on television. Perhaps they look up to another manager in the department and model themselves after that person.

Others make an attempt to imitate the archetypal manager who screams at their employees and tells them to "work harder!" Isn't it what you should be doing in this situation?

No, that is not the case. You've taken on one of the most challenging jobs possible by accepting the position of manager. It is a difficulty that is always there, yet it is different from the obstacles that you have faced in the past. Just like you, other people get promotions because they are competent at the tasks they do.

THE TRUE STORY BEHIND MY CAREER CHANGE

In my instance, the field of microbiology was one in which I excelled. My performance at work was above and above expectations. I was able to prepare samples and plate bacteria on agar plate medium more quickly than everyone else. I used to take a lot of satisfaction in the fact that regardless of how much work was assigned to me for the next week, I was always able to get it done.

My memory takes me back to the time when I was staring at a sample container. Testing the protein powders produced at the factories for the presence of Salmonella was one of our primary responsibilities. The powder and some water were combined in a jug that held four liters, and then the mixture was placed in an incubator. This was the first phase in the procedure. After a few of days, the bacteria in the powder would proliferate and produce a foul odor when they were released. After taking a sample, you would next transfer it into a selective medium so that the procedure could proceed. After the sample jug had been cleaned, refilled with sterile distilled water, and reprocessed, a fresh collection of samples would be used to start the testing procedure once again.

It had been a couple of years since I started working at the laboratory. I found out that people are wary of the activities that take place in the laboratory, which is one of the reasons why there aren't too many visitors. I can still recall the day when I asked myself, "How many times have I filled, incubated, and refilled this same jug? "Dozens, hundreds, or even thousands of times?" Who would've guessed? I got the distinct impression that I had arrived at a point of no further advancement, and I did not want to continue down this road.

Working in the laboratory was enjoyable, but at that same moment, I realized that if I kept doing what I was doing, it would eventually become my fate. The only possible advancement that would be open to me would be the post of lab manager; however, the person now holding that position was also young, so there was little prospect of my getting it. In addition, even if I were to get a promotion, what would my next step be after that?

I was aware that I needed to go, and given my circumstances, it was clear that I would be the one to initiate the departure.

Mentoring

Your responsibility as leaders is to foster the development of other capable leaders. The practice of servant leadership involves acting as a mentor to other people and directing them toward exemplary values. The information that is sent throughout this process is tailored specifically to the requirements of the mentee. Find a person whose leadership style you like and want to copy, and cultivate a connection with them. This will help you grow as a leader. This individual is going to be the most helpful companion for your trip. Your chances of becoming successful might be significantly increased by working with a mentor of high caliber.

What exactly is being a mentor?

The process of one person fostering the personal development and progress of another is known as mentoring. The mentor is the more experienced someone who works with the mentee, who is the less experienced person, to give direction or information via intellect, skills, or experience.

I have been fortunate enough to have a number of mentors in my professional life during the course of my career. These people have the potential to serve as your very own board of directors. My immediate boss, Jeff, has been a constant impact on me over the course of my career. He has helped me grow from a brand-new manager into the job that I now hold as clinical director over the biggest customer in our book of business. Jeff has been a tremendous asset to me. He has offered me with high-quality, constructive comments and has directed me down the route to gaining new managerial expertise. Who should you think about having as a guide or mentor?

Your mentors need to take a sincere interest in the advancement of your professional career. They should demonstrate abilities in careful listening and guide you down a route that leads to solutions. The person is obligated to keep your information secret and must have a strong commitment to your accomplishments. It's encouraging to hear that a familiar face is popping into your head. Mentoring is beneficial to the company, the persons being mentored, and the mentors themselves.

Competencies required of a mentor:

1. Possessing an open mind

2. listening with awareness

3. one who asks plenty of questions

4. Be truthful

5. Being conscious of oneself

There are several positive outcomes that might be expected for the company. Knowledge transmission, organized learning, the identification of high-potential employees, the cultivation of a corporate culture, and the refinement of soft skills are some examples of these.

Building connections, encouraging and fostering creativity, expanding one's network of professional contacts, improving one's coaching abilities, and experiencing more personal pleasure are some of the advantages that accrue to the mentor.

One of the advantages that might accrue to the person who is assigned as a mentee or who is assigned a mentor is the development of a new talent in the area of mentoring others. They improve their professional status, get an in-depth grasp of the company culture, and open up the possibility of acting as a mentor in the future.

Is learning to be a leader via a process called reverse mentoring the way of the future?

The millennial generation is responsible for disruptive innovation across the whole of every known company in the modern world. The business world has benefited from the Millennial generation's contributions of technology, new knowledge, and fresh points of view. The company would not be successful if it did not embrace innovation.

A novel approach known as "reverse mentoring" flips the traditional "top-down" learning model by having younger team members serve as mentors to high level executives. Businesses are coming up with novel and inventive applications for social media and technology in their operations. This kind of mentoring acts as a connection point for the two different people involved. These experienced mentors are educated on emerging forms of technology and culture. The junior mentor is provided with a career coach and a role model.

The mentorship connection, although in the other direction, is becoming more important in cultural sensitivity training. Both previous generations of collaborative relationships and forward-looking organizations have been bolstered as a result.

From Manager to Business Owner

I devoted many days to formulating a plan that outlined the procedures that I would have to carry out in order to assemble a convincing business case in order to determine whether or not the acquisition of the company would be possible from a monetary standpoint. I needed to provide a response to the issue of whether or not the website could function well as a standalone company, as well as the question of how much of an initial expenditure may be considered reasonable in order to purchase the website and get a standalone firm off the ground. I also realized that I needed a team of folks to engage in the job that lay ahead, on our own time, since our plates were going to be full merely from operating the company and completing the process of selling the property. The following three months were going to involve a large amount of work, but I was certain that the opportunity would be beneficial enough to warrant the time and effort that would be required to pursue it.

I approached Rob with the idea of expanding the team that was working on the sale process to include a leader for the site's operations (Steve), a quality and regulatory leader (Joe), and a finance leader (Chuck). Rob agreed to my proposal. To participate in the selling process, these duties were essential, and obtaining authority for them to do so would enable me to include them in my campaign to put together a proposal for us to acquire the property ourselves.

Walt and I had a conversation about my strategy, and although he was supportive of my decision to press through with it, he advised me to be extremely cautious about releasing it until I was completely prepared to react to the challenges I would face from the firm. I told Walt about my plan, and he gave me his blessing to do so. I was aware that if I was going to play the dual role of selling the site while also seeking to purchase it, I would need to maintain a delicate balance. Walt also conveyed to me that he was not interested in taking part in the effort to purchase the company, but that he would be supporting me in this endeavor.

I did ask him if he would be open to being appointed as part of the buying team, given that his tenure and expertise would be a helpful asset in assessing the credibility of our team, and he did say that he would be open to the idea. He gave his permission for me to use his name, but I was not to search for him to continue working at the site in the event that we were successful in acquiring it. The way ahead was decided upon by all of us. I was granted permission to include the other three members of the team in the sales process, and I was informed that I would be allowed to include them in the secondary goal that I was going to begin.

When I held the meeting with the new team members and conveyed the news, I realized that they needed to go through the same process of emotional adjustment that I had to go through in December when I was confronted with a dramatic shift. Before I invited them to join me for a meeting at the end of the day, I saw this situation develop over the course of many days.

I had prepared a few transparent slides prior to our getting together (this was a very long time ago, much before PowerPoint became commonplace in the business sector). I had calculated an estimate of the finances for the next five years, taking into account both favorable and unfavorable outcomes for the existing product portfolio that was being fulfilled by the website. Again, since we did not have Excel at the time, we had to rely on Lotus 1-2-3, which was the most efficient tool before Microsoft became the industry standard for business software.

The potential for cost savings that we had by "leaning" the processes, improving the processes to decrease variability, parametrically releasing goods (releasing them in real time), and getting rid of corporate overhead expenditures that had a substantial influence on the profit and loss statement was the clincher for the financial predictions. In addition to that, I discussed with them the company's Employee Stock Ownership Plan (ESOP), which was meant to guarantee that everyone who joined forces with us would have a minority part in the company as well as a heightened dedication to our achievement of success. This was something that I wanted to make sure everyone understood before they joined us. We discussed, came to an agreement on, and improved the top line business case and its effect on the bottom line over the course of three hours.

In addition, Chuck, who is in charge of finance, brought up the point that operating a stand-alone corporation would be entirely focused on cash, which he referred to as "shoe box accounting." The other two members of the team, including him, excitedly consented to become a part of the group. A non-disclosure agreement as well as a summary of our ownership agreements were also items that I had produced. Even though we had worked together for a number of years, I explained to them that I was of the opinion that writing down our agreement right from the start may prove to be extremely useful in the years to come. We decided to get together on Saturday of that week to map out the whole business case, and we all came to the conclusion that we would have a group discussion on a significant component of moving ahead, especially how we were going to fund our offer to acquire the company. We agreed that this would be the first step in moving forward.

During the following two months, in addition to doing our regular responsibilities, we were also required to host the dozens of members of the corporate team who came to visit our location. We all chuckled at the idea that the hotels and restaurants in our town must be going crazy because of the sudden and profitable increase in business and the amount of cash that seemed to have sprung out of nowhere. While everything was going on, and in our own time, we focused on honing and perfecting our company strategy.

We were able to identify genuine chances to cut costs and make advances in efficiency. We proposed a variety of ways in which the newly built and soon-to-be decommissioned pilot plant might be put to use, each of which would result in the creation of an entirely new source of income. We saw the possibility of lowering the existing supply costs that the firm was incurring for items sourced from the site in order to make our offering highly appealing to the commercial associates that work with us.

We spent a lot of time getting on the same page about how we would lead and how we would go about building the culture of our organization, and we all came to the conclusion that the contract manufacturing company we would be working with in the future would be quite different from the companies we had previously collaborated with. Specifically, we would disrupt the present pattern of offering contract manufacturing services in order to win the business, and then increasing the cost of supply with additional activities that were not included in the initial bids. This would allow us to save money. Permit me to elaborate...

In a nutshell, throughout the 1990s, the contract manufacturing sector of the pharmaceutical business was known for securing its foothold inside an innovative firm and then piling on extra costs one after the other. We came to the conclusion that we should provide a menu of services, each with its own pricing as well as a breakdown of our overhead expenses. The idea was founded on our view that our future customers would be best served if we were successful, and we intended to operate in a transparent, open-book relationship with our clients. In other words, we believed that our clients would benefit most from our success.

The process of selling the firm was coming to a conclusion; in three weeks, we were supposed to have a meeting to go through the finalist list of potential owners of the site. Fortunately, our business case and proposal were nearly ready for final approval, but there was still an important goal that needed to be achieved. In order to complete the acquisition, we need funding. We were aware of our company's history of selling manufacturing locations as part of a management buyout (MBO), which is when the current management teams were sold the firm together with continuous supply agreements for the low, low price of one dollar. Even though we had high hopes that this approach would be successful, the fact that the competition's finalists were being chosen was a clear indication that we needed to be ready to submit a competitive proposal.

I had to temporarily divert some of my attention away from my obligations for the firm in order to look into possible investment channels for the purpose of supporting our proposal. I approached large financial institutions located in the Carolinas, and we scheduled a week during which our team would go to Charlotte to present our case in person to three distinct financial institutions. We were encouraged by the state of the economy in the middle of the 1990s, as well as by the positive reactions we received from the financial institutions. During our time in Charlotte, cash was readily accessible, and we were given a warm welcome by all of the banks we visited. This was the case as we traveled from one bank to the next.

In the end, each bank expressed interest in some type of continuing cooperation with the company, and they were all adamant that the team maintain a minority stake and personally spend further capital. Ugh! The truth became clear to us when we sat down for our last night's meal, which consisted of drinks and burgers. Were we sure that becoming minority owners and agreeing to be governed by bankers who knew nothing about our company was something that we truly wanted to do?

The latest development has had me thinking about the possibility of a cooperation as well as the need for finances. I informed the team, "It is very evident that we cannot accomplish this by ourselves due to the funding that we want to put up. According to the calculations and projections that we carried out and checked, our company is capable of operating profitably with up to $7 million in additional funding.

I told them, "While we hoped we wouldn't have to take on that level of debt, we must be prepared to offer it even though we had hoped we wouldn't have to." Consequently, if we are destined to take on a partner, why aren't we able to choose who that partner would be, and why can't we find a partner who would have an interest in the firm that goes beyond merely funding?"

Understanding a topic, either on a theoretical or practical level, is the foundation of knowledge. The pharmacists who are responsible for mixing the compounds in your company need to have a wide understanding of therapeutic medications that may be used in animals and sold.

Experience is the practical knowledge or wisdom you receive as a result of what you have seen, seen, or gone through in your life. This is a test based on real-life scenarios. For instance, many ideas for marketing appear fantastic on paper and could even be successful in practice. However, successful marketers have a feel of the market since they have experimented with a variety of strategies throughout time. It's an instinct that's developed over years of experience.

Even though interpersonal connections are perhaps the most significant aspect of a person's talents, we don't always consider them to be among those capacities. There is a good reason why the old saying "It's not what you know, it's who you know" is still just as applicable now as it was back in the day. Having the appropriate connections paves the way for successful completion of tasks. This is not just true in terms of making sales, but also in terms of gaining access to necessary skills, generating finance, and overcoming obstacles posed by regulatory agencies.

The all-encompassing skill that basically encapsulates our strengths is referred to as talent. Even though the list is lengthy, some of the traits that are associated with talent include intelligence quotient (IQ), temperament, energy level, extroversion, creativity, reasoning, empathy, self-awareness, expressiveness, and so on. These talents are already programmed into our minds and bodies, and there is not much that can be done to develop them.

Why don't we undertake a speedy analysis of your top executives' abilities, knowledge, experience, and connections, as well as their talent?

Ryan said that it would be awesome if it didn't take too much time to complete.

We are able to do a comprehensive analysis. Before making any significant choices, it is necessary to do an in-depth study with the assistance of a trained professional coach.

Let's begin with Allison, your chief financial officer. What kinds of talents does a CFO at National need to have?

She has to be proficient in both accounting and financial analysis to be successful. The closing of the books, the compilation and analysis of the financial accounts, and the completion and filing of all reports with our creditors, the Internal Revenue Service, and other regulatory authorities are all responsibilities of our CFO. She also has a staff, therefore it is necessary for her to have the abilities necessary to encourage others in order to get things done in an atmosphere that can be described as somewhat chaotic.

Tom said that the list was rather adequate. Would you say that Allison has an expert level of those skills?

Without a question.

What about acquiring new information? Tom had inquired.

The requisite information goes hand in hand with the necessary abilities. For us to properly compile our financials in accordance with the regulations, our CFO has to have knowledge of GAAP as well as tax accounting. In addition to this, it is necessary for her to have an understanding of how our general ledger and the administrative systems that support it function. According to Ryan, she has to be proficient in accounting in addition to having an in-depth knowledge of credit agreements and the ability to use various financial models such as forecasting and net present value.

It seems like you have a wealth of information there. How does Allison's do in comparison?

Since Allie formerly worked for an accounting business, she possesses a strong understanding of GAAP accounting as well as the systems side of things. However, this is her first time dealing with a bank or a credit agreement, so it has been an educational experience for her. The credit agreement has its own set of accounting criteria for determining what should be included in the total amount of profit. I believe that this is the point when Allie may have made a mistake. Ryan said that despite this, she has intelligence and is making progress.

The answer is yes, one may acquire new information. provided that the individual have the necessary skills. It would seem that Allison is doing so.

Therefore, we have already discussed some of Allison's past experiences. In a broader sense, what kinds of experiences would be excellent for your Chief Financial Officer to have?

In hindsight, it seems that it would have been more beneficial for us to hire someone with prior experience working as a CFO rather than someone directly from an accounting company. We were not even considering taking on any debt at that point in time. During the time that we were negotiating the terms of the loan agreement, Allie seemed to be sipping from a fire hose. When we hired Mary, all we needed was a reliable accountant. She was just that. As I am certain that we will be able to pay off the debt, I believe that moving ahead, what we will need most is an experienced accountant.

People are micromanaged.

In order to achieve their full potential, individuals need to be inspired and motivated, and this is where leadership comes in. This may at times include leaders providing them with space so that they may do the tasks that they need to complete. A poor leader feels the need to maintain complete command over everything that is taking on under their watch. This requires the individual to practically look over the shoulders of everyone involved to ensure that things are being done to his or her standards.

Unfortunately, micromanaging may have a detrimental effect on an individual's level of productivity. When a person is in their "defense mode" almost every minute while working on a job, the activity becomes too stressful for them to complete. That individual won't be able to concentrate well on the job at hand because they will be preoccupied with how closely they are being observed. It's also possible that they dislike the leader for not trusting them or giving them enough liberty.

Leaders that engage in excessive micromanagement of their employees are often people who lack confidence in their own talents. They are hesitant to give up control because they are concerned about being overshadowed by the others that they are responsible for managing. Therefore, in order to guarantee that they would get credit for the accomplishments of the teams, they immerse themselves in every aspect of the operation.

Threatens Others or Acts As a Bully The populace

Fear is a tactic that is used by certain leaders and is one of their techniques. Although it could seem to be effective, doing so might really have quite a significant adverse effect. For instance, there are supervisors who have been known to threaten their staff with termination if they fail to do a job within the allotted amount of time. Although this does a good job of getting the staff excited about their work, it also makes for a highly stressful scenario. Because there is so much pressure on the staff, they have a greater propensity to make errors.

The quality of life of the workers is negatively impacted as well. Their irritability and lack of patience spill over into their personal life as a direct result of the stressful atmosphere in which they work. They have a propensity to alienate the people who provide them support, such as their friends and family.

Intimidation as a kind of leadership may undoubtedly have an effect not only on the members of the team but also on turnover rates. People who are bullied ultimately make the decision to quit their stressful leaders and go for ones that are more helpful.

Does not Put Standards Into Effect

People need to have a clear understanding of what is expected of them whether they are working on a project or their employment. If you have ever worked with people who do their own thing without being held responsible for their activities, then you are familiar with the impact that this may have on everyone else.

A leader who is not successful because they do not uphold the standards that have been established for a specific purpose is not an effective leader. These guidelines contribute to the preservation of both the quality and the numbers. The norms lose their relevance when people are not required to take responsibility for their actions. The performance will suffer, and as a result, the objectives will not be achieved.

Candidates who have passed the first stage of the interview process (no more than 30 or 40 percent) may be re-convened for a second interview to be attended by the Human Resources Department, but this time with the help of the head of the sector or division where the resource is to be placed. This interview may take place at a later date.

The second interview may start with a group discussion in which all of the applicants work together to solve a problem. This might be one possible format for the second interview. Two distinct teams might be formed and tasked with coming up with a solution within a certain amount of time.

This will allow you to evaluate how the candidates interact with one another, how they handle any issues that arise within a team, and which individuals seem to stand out more than others...

When it comes to making an overall assessment of everyone who was a part of this, all of this information will prove to be really helpful.

After that, each participant in the interview might proceed separately as follows:

1) Providing a detailed description of the function that you will be doing and the individuals with whom you will have close contact;

2) An examination of the candidate's particular competencies: you may design examinations on fundamental or specialized subjects that the applicant must be familiar with in order to be able to perform the duties of the post to the best of their abilities;

3) Ask the applicant a straightforward question like as, "How do you see

yourself in five years time within our company?"; it is not an easy question to respond to, and the responses will provide you with a great deal of information that is helpful to you;

4) The applicant will be given a description of the unfavorable parts of the task that needs to be done, with the intention of discouraging them and convincing them to quit up. Only in this manner will you be able to determine who is really interested in working for your firm, the individual in whom it will make sense to devote both time and financial resources in order to get the necessary training.

It should come as no surprise that there is no one method that can be used to organize an interview. The size of the firm, the kind of professional figure we are searching for (whether junior or highly qualified), the kind of contract we are offering... it should go without saying that the interview has to be set up and altered in accordance with each individual circumstance.

You will need to make an early sacrifice in terms of time, but this will be adequately repaid in the future, and the message I would want to get across is that if you can pick your employees properly, you will be halfway there. If you are able to do this, however, you will be halfway there.

Character and ability are necessary components for a successful leadership career. If you are in a position to recruit someone, it is ideal to find someone who has both of these qualities; however, if you are forced to make a decision, it is always preferable to go with resources that have character and then improve their talents by making sure that they are taught inside the firm over the course of many years.

People are glad to work on projects that excite them and interest them emotionally as well as professionally. It is important not to overlook how important it is to give each resource the appropriate function.

It is far simpler to hire the correct individuals for the job than it is to attempt to mold existing workers into more suitable positions.

How To Remain Consistent In A World That Is Constantly Changing

Have you ever seen the Jungle Book movie that Disney made?

When the four vultures have their discussion at the conclusion of the story, it's one of my favorite parts in the movie.

Someone yells out, "Hey, what are we going to do?"

The next line states, "I don't know. What are your plans for today?

The third member of the group then makes the recommendation that they check out the swinging part of the jungle.

The second participant then gives a response, saying, "Ah, things are right dead all over."

Following the denial of that proposition, the first vulture returns to the inquiry that was first posed.

"So, what do you wanna do?"

You may see a video clip at this link:

People will turn to you to make choices when you are in a leadership position. They are interested in learning what is scheduled to take place today. Where do we stand with this? In which path are we going to proceed? What are we doing this for?

You need to be able to provide answers to such inquiries in order to build your credibility as an authoritative figure.

Why do we have such a hard time accepting authority?

Those comical vultures are a representation of a widespread issue. Because there are so many options, we have lost our sense of excitement. Nothing really sticks out when one considers all the options available. There are many appealing alternatives, but you just cannot choose them all at this time. Therefore, you are unable to make a choice.

This demonstrates that you have not put any thought into how you want to spend your day before it has even begun. Therefore, you assess the situation at hand and focus on the most pressing matters. You might even choose to do something that isn't really productive but boosts your mood anyway. In any case, it is impossible to predict exactly where you will wind up.

And neither will your people know about it.

Maintain a Consistency

There is a more effective method for organizing your daily schedule.

You don't have to allow yourself to be blown about by the currents of chance and transformation. There is no need for you to question whether or not the decisions you've made are in fact the best ones. And if you think you have a fairly solid grasp on what to do, I'll show you how to grab on even more securely.

1. Determine what is significant and what is not significant.

Every leader has to be able to set priorities for their team.

That does not imply that you are good at it.

Or maybe it doesn't.

Shall we have a look at each one in turn, as you suggested?

For instance, if you are an alcoholic, one of your top priorities is probably to sneak a drink whenever and wherever you can get away with it. It's possible that it will impede your ability to carry out your responsibilities, but who gives a damn? You are unwavering in your commitment to this top priority.

Now, let's see who wins the coin toss.

If you're a person who gets things done, you'll be aware of the goals that your employer has assigned to you to accomplish. You are aware of the number of persons that will be required to assist you in completing the task. You are aware of the amount of time you have left. You can make room in your budget for unforeseen expenses.

Keeping all of this in mind, your top aim should be to concentrate as much as you possibly can on achieving those goals. You're going to make sure that your team chooses the appropriate activities at the appropriate times, aren't you?

That presents some challenges from time to time. However, it is impossible for anybody to get everything exactly flawless. Keep in mind that if you have a map, you will arrive at your destination much more quickly than if you do not.

2. Always stick to your guns and make choices that are in line with your previously outlined values.

Isn't this the most important factor in maintaining consistency?

Follow through with what you've promised. If you do that, everyone on your team will always know what to anticipate from you and they will be able to plan accordingly. They will realize the seriousness of your intentions. When they question you, they probably won't do so because they don't know the strategy; rather, it will be because they seek clarity on a particular aspect of it.

3. No matter what happens, you should never break your word and always keep your word.

The implication of this is easy to grasp.

You will have days when you just do not feel like working. Your daughter's first day of school is going to give you a lot of cause for concern. There is maybe an odd grinding noise coming from the vehicle. Your obnoxious first cousin is thinking about coming to stay with you for a whole month.

Everybody has a case of the blues once in a while.

The key is to not allow it to determine how you behave when you are at work.

You make your staff promise to leave their personal problems at the door when they come to work. What do you say? It is a sign of a mature leader that she is able to remain focused on her objectives in spite of the challenges that she faces in her personal life or in the job.

4. Determine in advance how you will deal with difficult situations and confrontations.

There are no certainties in life.

Your next breath will most likely arrive soon. On the other hand, it may not. The cargo that they guaranteed would be here today faces the possibility of a two-week delay. Even the simplest tasks are too difficult for the new employee you believed would be perfect for the position.

Although it is impossible to prepare for everything, it is possible to budget for unpredictability. You can probably guess what kind of inquiries individuals will have about the new regulations. You may prepare for periods of inactivity by having a backup plan. You have the ability to choose which boundaries the members of your team are permitted to cross and which they are not.

If you do that, you'll have something solid to lean on when the storms start rolling in.

The following is what will take place as a result of your consistency:

When members of your team are aware of what to anticipate from you, they will have increased feelings of safety. Even if they don't like you, they'll know they can believe what you say because of your reputation. They could even consider you to be vindictive, but they will never be able to accuse you of being unjust or imply that you are a liar.

Also, given that life already presents its fair share of unexpected events, you shouldn't make matters worse by being erratic and unable to make up your mind.

You may maintain your current degree of consistency by following these rules, regardless of how consistent you currently are. If you do that, you will be a strong leader in a world that is always changing.

What Actions Do You Hope Others Who Follow You Will Take?

After you have determined who your followers are, the next step is to articulate the goals that you have for them. The majority of the time, the organization decides what the objectives should be. You may be provided with the target sales figures or project goals by the corporation; nevertheless, you have the ability to modify them in accordance with your understanding of the capabilities of your followers.

Let's imagine the company wants you to increase the production of your team by a factor of two during the next month. You are conscious of the fact, though, that your group is capable of performing at a higher level. You have the ability to encourage the team to achieve results that are superior to those expected by the company.

On the other hand, if you believe that lowering the bar for your team is the best course of action, you are free to go in that direction. Take for example a college that is putting a lot of pressure on its basketball team to win the state championship. However, the coach is well aware that accomplishing such a feat with the squad in its present state is not conceivable. Instead of focusing on winning the competition, the coach encourages the squad to give it their all and earn valuable experience. When all of the players have the required amount of experience, they will have a higher chance of achieving their goals.

The organization's objectives shift in accordance with the stage of growth in which it is now operating. An organization that has just begun operations will need more labor. However, in comparison to more established firms, there will be a greater number of milestones reached by these startups. A person in this sort of leadership position will have less resources available to them. However, because of this, the expectations are far lower.

On the other side, a mature firm will have a greater need for managerial leadership as opposed to strategic leadership. It may be more vital to explore new markets, create new products, and change business culture in an older organization in order to revive the firm.

Taking Risks Is An Essential Component Of Effective Leadership

Taking risks is the first and most important stage in developing oneself into a leader from a more ordinary individual. There is a statement that goes, "no risk, no gain." This is a proverb. One interpretation of this saying is that individuals who do not possess the trait of being willing to take risks in life will undoubtedly find themselves among the masses. He will never be able to distinguish himself from the "other members of the crowd." Taking calculated risks is the trait that separates someone who "stands within the crowd" from someone who "stands out from the rest of the crowd." Listed below are some examples that illustrate the key distinction between the two:

Example A: You had to switch buses at the bus stop on your way to the workplace since you missed your first bus. You are startled to find a swarm of people gathered around something. When you go to investigate what is going on, you find a guy who is covered in blood and seems to have recently been involved in an accident. If he is not sent to the hospital as soon as possible, he will not survive his injuries. You will be presented with two options: As a responsible citizen, you should take the guy to the hospital immediately.

maybe you could just go to the office since it has nothing to do with you anyhow.

If you give it some thought, you realize that you also had a third option available to you: you could have joined the throng, observed what was going on, and let the guy face whatever destiny was in store for him. Is this a trait that a genuine leader should have? It is not the case at all. You are just an average person, yet you had the opportunity to distinguish yourself from the other people in the throng and could have assisted the guy. If you did so and picked the first choice, then you are a hero, a leader who has the bravery to stand out from the crowd glaringly. If you did not choose the first option, then you are not a hero. In the event that you did not do so and instead stood among the throng, then it is impossible to distinguish you from the "rest of the crowd."

Permit me to provide you with a more illustration:

Example B: You are on your way to the market when all of a sudden you notice someone drowning in the pond that is located in your hamlet. Because there is no one else around who can assist the kid or lady who is drowning, you have the opportunity to exit your vehicle, go to the water, and rescue the child or woman from drowning. You are not to blame for the drowning of the individual, and no one else can see you standing by and doing nothing to save the person who is drowning. Therefore, you have the option of claiming that it is none of your concern, as the situation is not your responsibility. You will also have the following two options available to you in this circumstance:

Ignore the plight of the poor guy.

or

How are you going to be able to assist him while you are on your way to the market?

If you choose to ignore the plight of the boy and do nothing to save him, you will be considered a member of the mob whether or not anybody is observing you or there is a large group of people around. If, on the other hand, you assisted the youngster, people would remember you more than the "rest of the crowd" because of your actions.

In situations like these, if you assist the less fortunate or those in need, even if it means putting your own life in danger or taking the chance of running into the authorities, as in the first example, then you undoubtedly have the qualities necessary to become a leader. If you did not, then you do not possess the characteristic that is necessary to become a leader; it is as simple as that.

The vast majority of individuals will not take the risk because they either feel embarrassed of themselves or they are terrified of the prospect of taking the risk. Those who have leadership traits or who want to become leaders rather than ordinary men would assist the needy and those who are experiencing a crisis. This demonstrates that they have the attribute of being willing to take risks, which is the first step toward becoming a leader.

You will have a good grasp on who you are in real life if, when confronted with a circumstance that is analogous to what you find in real life, you choose to do nothing more than blend in with the crowd. You will also learn what aspects of yourself are lacking and have been holding you back from developing into a genuine leader.

You are keeping yourself from doing a fantastic thing and taking a risk for a good cause, which is a trait that stands for a genuine leader if you feel guilty of helping the needy because you believe that you don't even know that person. If you think that you don't know that person, then you are preventing yourself from doing a great thing. You walk away in an egotistical manner because you lack the intestinal fortitude to face the consequences of your actions and either run away from the truth or simply escape it by making up stupid excuses. This is what sets you apart from others who are in leadership positions. If, on the other hand, you believe that you would have behaved differently under the same circumstances, then you are unquestionably progressing toward being a leader.

If you did not assist the guy in need, another possible explanation for your actions is that you were too terrified to do so. You could have had the notion that, in the event that you assisted in the situation, and the guy passed away as a direct result of your actions, the authorities would point the finger of blame at you. What would you do if you were forced to shoulder all of the responsibility for the other person? You may also be under the impression that if you were to assume the obligation of admitting the individual to the hospital, you would be required to spend a significant amount of money. Who can say for sure that you won't have to assume responsibility for the guy and his family?

It's possible that you've encountered a number of inquiries quite similar to these, all of which point to the fact that you're scared and explain why you've developed an attitude that tries to escape reality.

These examples are presented only for the purpose of demonstrating to you what it is like to deal with challenging circumstances and then act responsibly. If you are really committed to making the world a better place for other people, then you won't ever make an effort to hide from the truth. You are going to follow your instincts and act in accordance with what your heart tells you. You will just like putting yourself in potentially dangerous situations, and once you have done it once, you will want to do it again and again, which will enable you to discover the leader that lies dormant within you. You will be able to see the difference and will have the ability to bring about the change on your own.

In the event that you believe you are incapable of doing dangerous duties and that you can just act as a sheep in the herd, taking only one such dangerous initiative will make you brave and courageous enough to differentiate yourself from the crowd. You may have previously had the mentality of a sheep, but with only one step, you will create the attitude of a lion inside you.

As was said before, a good leader should have the confidence and bravery of a lion, two qualities that are essential to effective leadership. Therefore, you have to realize that the only way for a leader to become fearless is to take chances, and that this is how the first historical chapter begins. Taking risks is a skill that transforms a person into a great leader. This is especially true of an individual who has the guts to stand out in a crowd.

A person is not required to put himself at danger just in the scenarios described above. There are a lot of different ways to put yourself in danger. The following are some more opportunities to demonstrate your worth:

You have undoubtedly betrayed your fellow man if, despite having enough money to spend on luxury products, you hesitate before giving even a little sum to a charitable organization. You could spend hundreds or thousands of dollars on a high-end designer garment or spend more than a regular person's yearly income on a luxury automobile, believing that it is your money and that you have the right to use it anyway you want, but giving even 1% of it puts you in a position where you have to make a tough choice. In such case, we would want to inquire as to whether or not you really know what actions a leader should do in a predicament such as this one. A leader never shows fear or avoidance of any opportunity to assist the needy and those who are less fortunate. In point of fact, a leader is always ready to provide a hand to those in need.

A good leader should not be afraid to put themselves in dangerous situations or to coach others who do not have the self-assurance to do the same. In this manner, a leader may also brighten the lives of others under their charge. Be the light first if you want to show others the way, because if you don't, you'll never be able to be the one who can lead others successfully. So, before you try to teach others the way, become the light yourself.

Getting Ready to Influence Others

If you take the time to apply each of these stages, you will always be ready when you come across that particular individual or when opportunity comes your way. There are a few important easy processes and parts to preparing to prepare to convince, and they may be broken down into many categories. It is said that opportunity meets preparedness at just the right time, and this is the kind of preparation we are discussing here.

The first step is to gather as much information as possible on your target demographic, often known as the group of individuals with whom you will be engaging in conversation. When you go to a conference, one of your goals should be to find out what the other attendees have in common with you. When you go to a nightclub, you should try to figure out what attracts all of these different individuals together. What do they take pleasure in? What are some of their shared characteristics? This is the first stage of the research process. In addition to that, when you pick certain individuals, you then investigate their unique past and the things that they like doing.

The second step in being ready is to research your case and become an expert in the message you want to give. This is important regardless of whether you want to persuade others to work with you or to join you and establish an alliance with you over a political or environmental problem. When someone has more knowledge about your topic than you have, it is hard to convince them of anything. It's just as crucial to have depth of knowledge as it is to have charm.

You need to not only be aware of everything that is good about your stance, your project, your perspective, and your argument, but you also need to be aware of everything that may be said against it. When you initially start learning sales as a skill, one of the first things you'll learn is how to overcome the most common objections. There are certain arguments that are only empty phrases that don't carry any weight, while there are other points that are very challenging to refute. When you're in sales, one of the most challenging arguments to overcome is "I have to ask my husband; I have to ask my wife; I'm not allowed to make financial decisions on my own." This is because women are more likely to say that they are restricted from making independent monetary choices by their partners. This is a difficult obstacle to overcome, and you will need to wait till the other person is there before you can do so. You should be able to handle the majority of the other objections on the spot. "I'm not really sure I can afford it; I'm not ready to buy right now; I'm not sure if I want this; I don't know if I need a new car; I'm not sure if this meets my needs." "I don't know if I need a new car; I'm not sure if this meets my needs." These are low-level objections, and the way you respond to them will determine whether or not you are successful in closing the deal.

When you're trying to raise money for a good cause, one of the most typical things people say is, "Why should I give to you instead of someone else? What makes your organization different from other charitable organizations? The more you are aware of the challenges you will encounter and the more you are prepared for them, the simpler it will be to conquer those challenges. You can't rely on yourself to come up with excellent responses in the heat of the moment. Why put in more effort when you can just work smarter instead? Every argument has holes in it somewhere. There is a significant issue here if you think that the validity of your argument cannot be questioned in any way. You are not seeing the same things that others perceive. I come into contact with folks on a regular basis who have unwavering conviction in their position and insist that "I'm one hundred percent correct. Everyone agrees with what I have to say." Despite this, around fifty to sixty percent of the populace does not share their viewpoint. If what you're saying is true, then everyone on earth should agree with you. However, even in this day and age, there are still some individuals who hold the belief that the planet could be flat.

There will always be some who see flaws in the reasoning you provide. The secret to being successful is to recognize potential gaps in your argument, as well as objections raised by others and your own, and be ready to provide a response. You can go beyond research by looking into individuals's past activities, which is particularly useful if you are considering political or greater levels of influence and if your goal is to influence large groups rather than individual people. How did this population segment vote in elections in the past? Which political concerns do they prioritize, and what are those concerns? What exactly are their concerns? Do they have any concern about employment? Do they have any regard for the natural world? Do they give a damn about the crime rate?

Every organization has its own unique set of priorities, and the primary activity of political parties in every nation is to conduct surveys, surveys, and more surveys. They look at information from the past. They continue to pose inquiries throughout time. They are interested in learning what you consider to be the most pressing concern, and that is the topic that they will discuss with you. People speak about employment a lot in this neighborhood since so many people are seeking for work. In a neighborhood where everyone is affected by the same issues with crime, people speak about the crime. No matter what the problem is in the region, this becomes the most salient point in their case when presented to the people who live there.

In addition to this, you might investigate the particular reasons why this individual or this audience reacts negatively to the issue. Everyone is going to be feeling the effects of the economy if a plant in the town has just closed down. This is going to be something that is particularly on their mind, especially if there was a significant increase in crime not too long ago or if someone was let free on a technicality after committing some serious crimes. It is much simpler to connect with individuals when you have a solid understanding of the exact reasons behind why they feel so passionately about certain problems.

The things that are important to me change as time goes on. When something significant occurs in my family, the priorities that were crucial a few months ago could shift. When someone falls ill, receiving proper medical treatment unexpectedly vaults to the top of the priority list. individuals who have had cancer themselves or have had a family member who has had cancer are considerably more enthusiastic about the illness and have a much different feeling about it than individuals who are against cancer in general. This is despite the fact that we are all aware that cancer is a significant issue. There isn't a single person who supports cancer, but there is a wide range of attitudes about the disease, from "I'm against cancer" to "I'll do whatever it takes. Because of the impact that cancer has had on my life, I am willing to contribute financially as well as my time to the battle against the disease. Calibration will be easier for you if you know your audience and take the time to provide this information.

The joke is one last strategy that does not work when it comes to being ready to convince someone of anything. Traditional speech classes usually educate their students to begin their speeches with a joke or to have a joke prepared for their audience. If you don't conduct research on your audience, you run the risk of making a joke that falls flat on its face. We now live in a world in which, if you say a joke that bombs, doesn't hit correctly, or is misinterpreted, it ends up on Twitter, and it becomes a defining moment in your life, even when people are plainly misinterpreting what you said. This is the case even when people are clearly misinterpreting what you said.

People in this day and age are seeking for any reason to value signal on Twitter and say something along the lines of, "Look, I found someone doing something wrong, and now I'm pointing it out to prove I'm good because they are bad." That plays a significant role in our cultural traditions. People sign up for Twitter because they didn't bother to do any research beforehand. There are some jokes that are better suited for particular audiences. There are several jokes that are OK in the United States but might get you jailed in England, and vice versa. Those jokes also apply in reverse. Your ability to deliver a joke that doesn't go over well depends on your familiarity with the history and culture of your people.

Exchange of information

The ability to communicate effectively is a crucial component of leadership. Open lines of communication are established by effective leaders and kept open by them. This is a channel of contact that goes in both directions and encourages coworkers to provide information. It is in no way a strict, top-down, hierarchical flow of demands from the leader. The most successful leaders motivate their teams to perform at their best by providing them with attainable objectives and clear instructions on how to reach those goals. At the same time, they put the members of the team under pressure to provide the greatest performance they are capable of giving. It is necessary for leaders to sometimes operate outside of their comfort zones in order to inspire followers to do the same. They encourage employees to make choices on their own and provide them the authority to make decisions when it is necessary.

Dedicated effort

Strong leaders inspire loyalty in their followers. It is not so much devotion to the leader as it is dedication to the goals that the organization as a whole has established for itself. A personality-based blind allegiance that inhibits conversation and expects members of the team to obey commands without questioning them may lead to negative outcomes for the team. Trust is an essential element in effective leadership. Both the members of the team and the leader need to have the conviction that the other party can be trusted, and the members of the team need to have the conviction that the leader can trust them. The ability to win the support of one's team is essential to effective leadership. When communicating with the members of the group about what has to be done, it is critical to ensure that they fully get the "why we are doing this." When people are aware of the reasons behind the significance of performing a certain action, they are more strongly motivated to execute that action. Because of this, the leader is responsible for sharing knowledge in the proper manner. Does this imply that the group must listen to all that the leader has to say? Not at all, in fact. It implies that there must be a enough amount of transparency to keep the team moving in the direction of the objectives set for the group.

Cooperative effort

Effective leaders encourage teamwork and keep the lines of communication open. It is just as vital to listen to what the other members of the team have to say as it is to tell them what needs to be done. Everyone on the team will feel more invested in the choices if they are given the opportunity to voice their concerns, objections, and recommendations. If the members of the team believe that they were given a chance to contribute input before the final choice was made, they will be more likely to accept the decision made by the leader and to follow the orders even when they disagree with the conclusion that was made. Strong leaders are adept at delegating responsibility to their subordinates. The concern that the other person will not do the assignment in the same way as the leader would have is a common reason for leaders to be hesitant about delegating critical responsibilities. Since the world is continually evolving, wise leaders always remain flexible and adaptable to new circumstances. challenges will arise that both the leader and the team had not anticipated; thus, in order to overcome these new challenges, it may be necessary for them to adopt a different mentality, and they may need to seek for new approaches to address the problem.

When you transfer duties to your subordinates during the course of your career, you come to realize that they may not complete the tasks in the same manner in which you could have done them. On the other hand, you made sure they understood the intended result, and they were aware that you would follow up to ensure that the objective was reached. You come to the realization that they often came up with solutions to the issue that were superior to those you would have thought of, either in terms of effectiveness, cost, or both.

The Management of Stress

Control the amount of stress in your life. It is futile to approach a social meeting with the expectation of having a positive outcome if one does not practice effective stress management. The capacity to have productive conversations and interact with others may be severely hindered by stress. When you're under a lot of pressure, you're more likely to misunderstand and misinterpret the signals that other people are sending you, and vice versa. Emotions are very infectious, and the way you behave and act may have a negative impact on the individuals in your immediate environment.

When you're in a bad mood, you run the danger of making other people feel bad as well. When you are furious, your words and actions might make other people upset as well. If you are feeling overburdened by stress, the most effective thing for you to do in this scenario is to give yourself a break. Take a break from the stressful event or discussion and wait to return when you are ready and have recovered your calm.

Communication that is Clear and Concise

Many of us are all too acquainted with the experience of having difficulty communicating and making ourselves understood clearly and in sufficient detail. This is the reason why we refer to it as a "skill." If it were simple, we would all be able to have engaging conversations and be adept at social interaction. When you need this talent to pitch a new project at work, lock in a new customer, or even get yourself the job you've been eyeing during an interview, it can be a real challenge to struggle to express the message correctly. This is particularly true when you need this skill to land yourself the job you've been eyeing.

Like other social skills, effective communication is something that can only be honed by repeated practice. Work is another element of your life where social skills and the ability to communicate effectively are essential, in addition to the social contacts you have on a more frequent basis. In a more professional situation, there is a lot going on. It's a chaotic situation where people are racing about trying to get things done, there are deadlines that need to be reached, there are meetings to attend, and everyone is trying to collaborate, assign jobs, and make sure that everything is finished on time before the end of the day. Due to the nature of the surroundings, communication may prove to be difficult at times. It is much more difficult to keep your communications straightforward and to the point.

There are instances when you just have a few short minutes to convey your point, to keep someone's attention long enough to have an effect. Nobody has the time to spare, and even if they had, they wouldn't be interested in investing a lot of time trying to figure out what it is that you're trying to convey. Keeping your communication as simple as possible in a world filled with so many opportunities for distraction, noise, and clutter is often the strategy that will prove to be the most fruitful.

There are two significant obstacles that need to be cleared before successful communication can be achieved. The first thing you should do is try to make your communications as brief as you can so there is no chance for mistake. The second step is getting over your fear of being among other people. Let's go to work and overcome the first obstacle that stands in our way.

Keeping Things to a Minimum

This is going to be your greatest opportunity of retaining the attention of your audience for a sufficient amount of time for your efforts to be successful. For a social relationship to be effective, it is essential that both parties understand one another. Especially if you find yourself in a position of authority and responsibility. It is essential for a leader to have the communication skills necessary to simplify their communications, since this increases the likelihood that the majority of their followers will comprehend what they are trying to convey.

If your followers are unable to understand what it is that you are attempting to convey to them or the actions that you want them to do, you cannot be considered a successful leader. People in this day and age have even less free time than they had in the past since we live in a fast-paced environment. In today's fast-paced world, you won't have more than a few precious minutes to create a good impression on people. When you aren't hurrying from one work to the next, it takes even less time to talk face to face with others. Maintain a straightforward and uncomplicated manner of speech when communicating, and go right to the point. Maintain a straightforward approach using the following strategies:

Communicate Clearly Ensure that you speak at a speed that is comfortable for you and that you pronounce each word. Avoid hurrying since doing so puts you at danger of having your words run together too much, making it difficult for your audience to understand what you are trying to convey. Additionally, steer clear of employing slang or jargon, since some of the phrases you use may be foreign to some of your listeners. When you comes to discussing a potential business transaction with a customer, it is particularly astute to keep this one in mind. When making selections, the customer will often base their judgments on how well they can comprehend what you are saying. In the end, this is what sways their decision to agree with us.

Communicate With Each Other As Equals - Communicate with other people as though they are on the same level as you. Try to avoid treating someone as though they are below you in social standing. You are not required to speak to them as if they are superior to you, either. Instead, you should strive to speak to them in a way that is respectful and equal to you. Before you even make an effort to communicate, you should give some thought to the audiences that you will be interacting with. Which language do they feel most comfortable communicating in? What is it that they will react to and feel the strongest connection to the most?

Straight to the use: When you're pressed for time, there's no use in dancing about the issue; you have to get to the heart of the matter. One essential ability that all effective communicators possess is the awareness of how critical it is to get straight to the point as fast as possible. Even though you have a lot that you want to convey, you should condense it down to simply the most important points. When you go right to the point, you not only keep the attention of the people in your audience for much longer, but your message is also absorbed in a much more efficient manner. Mastering the art of summarizing your most important ideas and then limiting yourself to discussing those points alone is an essential skill for keeping things succinct.

Repeat and Reinforce is the practice of repeatedly repeating the most important aspects of your message in order to bolster its impact and ensure that it fully registers in the recipient's mind. Information is processed differently by different people at different rates. It's possible that some individuals need several instances of reinforcement and repetition before they ultimately understand it. This may be accomplished considerably more quickly and easily if you reduce your communications to a minimum.

Reduce Your Word Count Simply using fewer words can help simplify the process of repetition and reinforcement. Use fewer words, but make sure you're picking the proper ones. When you say less, you use less time, which cuts down on the amount of time that you use, which then provides more free time for your receiver to ask any questions that they need to in order to clarify your points. When you say less, you cut down on the amount of time that you use. Before you speak, it is helpful to write down what you are going to say on paper beforehand. When you put it in writing, you are able to examine the structure of each phrase and make a note of the sentences that you believe are far too lengthy. Where are the opportunities to use fewer words? Or might it be rephrased in such a way that it could be conveyed in three words rather than five?

The Importance Of Actions And Movements

"People will remember you for the things that you accomplish. The activities that we partake in are the most significant aspects of all. They outlive our finite existence. The things that we accomplish are similar to monuments that people construct in commemoration of heroes after they have passed away. Similar like the pyramids that the Egyptians erected in their pharaohs' honor." This is a quote from the character August who appears in the novel Wonder. The story is about a little kid who has been homeschooled by his mother up to the fifth grade because of the terrible facial disfiguration he was born with. It is taught in primary schools around the nation. Because he takes such immense pleasure in his profession, he is able to approach school with the self-assurance necessary to withstand the constant harassment he is sure to encounter there.

Along the same lines as Auggie in Wonder, the more you are able to give your kid agency in their responsibilities, the more they will be able to tolerate and maneuver through challenging social circumstances.

Your kid has spent the last five years participating in substantial movement, which has helped them strengthen their gross and fine motor abilities. They have learned how to pick up a little object, stir, pour, lift items, jump, leap, dance, and perform cartwheels, among other things. They learn what their bodies are capable of accomplishing with each movement they make, as well as what activities they really like performing with their bodies. Unbelievably, this revelation in movement creates the framework for them to find the purpose of their existence, which is discussed in Chapter 11.

You are going to find out what kinds of activities your kid enjoys doing, what kinds of responsibilities you can hold them responsible for, and what kinds of things they become extremely excellent at.

SERVICE OF THE BHAKTI

Bhakti yoga literally translates to "devotional service," and the Bhakti scriptures teach us how to move our bodies in a Zen-like manner. Movements of the body, activities that engage the senses, and a compassionate connection to one's Inner Parents, the cosmos, and the community are all components of service. This service satisfies the requirements of free will and agency to an excellent degree. If your kid views the completion of activities as service rather than a job or duty, they will feel more fulfillment from the experience.

The inner sanctum, also known as the pujari chamber, can be found at the Kalachandji temple that is located in Dallas. This little but potent room, which exudes a great amount of spiritual energy, is where all of the sacred objects and objects used in worship are stored. In this location, hundreds of priests collaborate closely with one another while maintaining perfect harmony. From three forty-five in the morning until nine thirty in the evening, there are a thousand minor jobs that are finished. Detailed instructions are provided for each and every activity. The objects used in worship are seen as manifestations of deity and are thus accorded a great value. Absolutely nothing falls, bangs, or scrapes against the floor. Each item is handled with care as it is positioned in its appropriate location, whether it be on a shelf, in a drawer, or on a tray. Hand-held bells, water glasses, little spoons, lights, and miniature trays are among the items that are used regularly. When they are being cleaned or polished, the water temperature should be exactly perfect (neither too hot nor too cold), and they should not be scraped with too much force. Every activity, as well as everything that has to be done in order to finish that activity, is a purposeful, love-filled contact with the body and surroundings, and it is done in the spirit of service. Participating in this activity will provide you with an unforgettable experience.

Bhakti literature instruct us that our homes should be seen as extensions of temples. We have a respectful attitude toward the task that has to be done, and we show reverence to all of the materials that are brought into it. In this frame of mind, you should revere both

the work and the play that your kid does.
Do not consider it a pointless use of your
time.

The Role Of The Brain In Determination

We are often sent to emergency situations with little information other than an address, which isn't always accurate. In some instances, we don't even have that. When we get at the site, we are often greeted by agitated individuals who are shouting that it took us thirty minutes to get there and that we need to take action. In a letter to his wife, Major General George G. Meade stated the following after the Gettysburg Campaign in 1863: "The most difficult part of my work is acting without correct information on which to predicate actions."30

I continued my studies on the subject, and I started giving presentations and leading discussions on decision-making to my shift. Following one of my classes, I had a conversation with a lieutenant who voiced their exasperation with a number of the challenges that we confront when we get on the scene of an incident. My response was, "Hey! Accept and revel in the anarchy! We react to crises in a world where there is a lot of chaos and uncertainty.

Even though I had read quite a few books and articles on the topic of decision-making, it wasn't until 2009 that I gained a significant amount of new knowledge on the topic. My training at the National Fire Academy (NFA) in Emmitsburg, Maryland, began in September of that year, and it was there that I was accepted into the four-year Executive Fire Officer Program. The curriculum is geared for senior fire officers and offers classes in Executive Development, Executive Analysis of Fire Service Operations in Emergency Management, Executive Leadership, and Community Risk Reduction. Although the NFA has since reorganized the curriculum, when I participated, the on-campus portion of each class lasted for a total of two weeks. Following the conclusion of each course, I was given a period of six months to successfully complete an applied research project (ARP) before moving on to the next academic year. In addition, completion of the fourth-year Advanced Research Project (ARP) with a passing grade was necessary in order to graduate from the program.

My first Advanced Role Playing challenge was to make rapid tactical decisions while under pressure. The study identified the elements that contribute to stressful decision-making and provided recommendations on how to enhance the decision-making process.31 The Situational Awareness at the Command Level was the subject of my second actionable recommendation pertaining to the issue.32 The information that was obtained from both study studies shed light on the functioning of the brain throughout the decision-making process. In addition, the investigation exposed how little I really understood about the topic and how much more there is for me to learn about it.

Every day, we make a number of choices, the most majority of which are made instinctively or with very little consideration. When Joe Schmuckatelli takes the elevator to the top level of the Sears Tower in Chicago, he doesn't stand there and look at the buttons, wondering what to do with them. Joe takes less than a second to look at, select, and press the button that corresponds to the floor that he wants to go to in the elevator. On the way back, he presses the button that has the arrow pointing in the other direction. After the door has opened, Joe enters the elevator and presses the "G" button, which is the button for the bottom floor. The next thing that he hears is a ding! The door swings open, and Mr.Schmuckatelli descends to the street level, where he will proceed to buy a renowned Italian sandwich made in the Chicago way. The choice between the two options was an easy one to make as long as the elevator didn't become stopped between levels.

Marriage, job choices, medical treatment alternatives, and big financial decisions are examples of the kind of decisions that call for more time, contemplation, and prayer. In times like this, we have the luxury of taking stock of the situation and thinking through the implications of various courses of action. On the other end of the scale are occupations that involve significant levels of stress and need quick, important decision-making while the employee is functioning under intense strain.

It's possible that you're thinking, "Rick, I don't fly planes, fight fires, arrest people, or perform surgery." And you'd be right. The question is, "How does all of this business with making snap decisions affect me?" If you drive a motor vehicle on a public street or highway, you will always have to make split-second judgment calls to avoid colliding with other cars, pedestrians, or items that are located on the route. In the event that your niece, who is just two years old, is speeding toward the flooded drainage ditch, you are going to have to make a quick choice in order to halt her. Every individual who walks the surface of the planet will eventually run across circumstances that need them to make snap decisions.

According to the findings of my study, the following factors have an effect on our capacity for decision making:

The current condition of both our body and mind

Are you hungry, fatigued, or feeling unwell?

What kind of attitude do you have—a good one, or a negative one? Do you have bravery, or do you have fear?

Levels of education, training, and practical experience

Is there a sphere that dominates the others?

Will these three factors be beneficial to you or will they be detrimental?

The three qualities of knowledge, talent, and ability

How self-assured are you, exactly?

Do you acknowledge the constraints you face?

The conditions and the setting in which we find ourselves.

Exist potential risks to your health, safety, career, income, and other aspects of your life?

Is it calm and collected around the decision-making process, or is there a lot of confusion?

The currently available data

What do you know about the present predicament and its associated conditions?

How reliable is the information that you provided?

The pressure brought on by not knowing

How well do you perform when you're under pressure?

Will things grow better or worse for you in the future?

Time that is available

Is there a pressing need to make a choice right now?

Is time working for you or against you?

The importance of the choice at hand

Who will be affected by the choice you make?

What will change as a result of your decision?

Awareness of the situation

What is the amount of perception and comprehension that you have about the situation?

Are you able to guess what will go place after this?

How Can You Ensure That The Recruitment Process Is Aligned With Your Purpose?

First, as a recruiter, you need to make sure that you are able to properly communicate the objective of the business and that you are upfront with it in every contact with a prospect. Second, draft or encourage the drafting of detailed but succinct position descriptions, and ensure that the appropriate questions are posed to the client at the very outset of the search process. In far too many cases, job descriptions are ambiguous and do not include the mission of the organization anywhere in the text. Worse yet, if a posting is constructed from such a description, it may very likely attract individuals with various aims, many of which will not coincide, so squandering important time spent recruiting. Third, make sure you ask your prospects and candidates the correct questions to determine whether or not they are related to your organization's overall mission. Listed below are some ideas to consider:

"What did the company that you most recently worked for do to further its mission?"

"Did the mission of that particular firm move you in any way? If not, then why not?"

"Which of these could serve as a source of motivation for you?"

Last but not least, you should interact with the prospects in a variety of different ways and spend time with each of them. You will have a better understanding of the applicants' purposes and ideals if you engage with them more.

Finding the candidate with the most impressive résumé from a pool of candidates is no longer a priority during the leadership recruitment process. Today, the primary objective of this approach is to identify extraordinary leaders, which, from the perspective of the firm, implies achieving alignment not just on performance but also on purpose. It should not be confused with the practice of recruiting for "culture fit." A company's culture may be summarized as "how" the company does business. The concept has been deeply ingrained in recruitment for a considerable amount of time and has become the cornerstone of many corporate recruiting procedures. On the other hand, it has recently taken on a more tribal connotation, which may be summarized as those who "look like us, think like us, work like us, and live like us." There is a high risk of discrimination occurring throughout the recruiting process if it is based on an ill-defined concept of cultural compatibility. It has been weaponized in some companies and turned into a word that interviewers use as a catchall term to exclude individuals from consideration. Reframe "culture fit" as "culture-add" (those who connect with the "why" of the organization or its goal), and look for applicants who contribute to the culture rather than those who just fit into it. This results in companies having cultures that are both more rich and varied.

According to NeelieVerlinden of AIHR, the following are the advantages that may be gained through aligning purpose early on in the process:

A lower rate of turnover: If you recruit someone who is compatible with the goals of the firm as a whole and the core principles that underlie it, they will have a far stronger desire to remain an employee there for a significant amount of time. This indicates that in order to achieve exceptional results in recruiting, recruiters should place equal emphasis on a candidate's job fit and their purpose fit. Recognizing both, but making purpose fit the focus throughout the recruiting process can help you lay the groundwork for a reduced percentage of employee turnover.

Improved quality of hire: workers who have a sense of belonging in the company for which they are employed report higher levels of happiness, which in turn has a beneficial effect on their level of engagement and productivity. They will need less time to become fully functioning, and while they are doing so, they will enhance the morale of their coworkers.

Purpose would be one of the elements in a top-secret formula for increasing employee engagement; however, there is no such thing as a secret recipe for employee engagement. People who work for an organization that shares their beliefs and whose mission inspires them will do their jobs with a great deal more zeal and enthusiasm than those who don't recognize themselves in the organization in which they are employed.

Productivity is raised as a result of all of these factors, which is a direct result of higher employee productivity.

Stronger recommendations: Referrals from current staff members have always been one of the most effective methods for finding new candidates. Referrals often have a higher rate of operational efficiency, greater levels of productivity and engagement, and a longer tenure with the organization. You should handle this carefully, and it must be done correctly, or otherwise it might be a method for accidentally lowering the representation of underrepresented groups in the organization. If you manage it well, however, you can avoid this happening.

Candidates that are naturally interested will be able to make the connection between the company's purpose and their own if the recruiting process includes a test of their belief and enthusiasm for the organization's mission. Candidates will also be given more influence from the beginning thanks to the establishment of a more sophisticated talent acquisition procedure that will assist the expansion of the firm. If the company's recruiters are successful in instilling the company's mission and values in the individuals they employ from the very beginning of the selection process, then the company will always have a purpose that is both present and active.

When a company is driven only by profit, power, or bureaucracy, there is a significant risk that its personnel would develop a mentality of "job" and labor just for financial compensation. Peter Drucker, a renowned authority on management, famously said that "to make a living is no longer enough, work also has to make a life." People are searching for this sense of meaning in their professional lives. We strongly suggest that you include a genuine message about your goal into every recruitment interaction. Since it is up to you to connect the dots, you should look for ways in which the candidate's goals align with those of the company. Individual, team, and organizational purpose can seem like an excessive amount of purposes, but in reality, it's simply a process of developing a single narrative line that helps candidates understand how they fit into the greater picture.

"What's Good, Right Here And Right Now?"

It was originally believed that the ancient Buddhist sages found the method of moving away from the views of the first sort of person (everything processed as good fortune or misfortune) via years, even decades, of meditation. However, this is no longer the case. This process would (ideally) conclude in "enlightenment" about embracing the transience that is inherent in life and finding delight in it.

In the beginning of my career as a coach, I was neither a practitioner of meditation nor a student of positive psychology. Nevertheless, I was really lucky to have a coach who was, and as a result, my own personal version of "enlightenment" started to take place after just a few number of coaching sessions with him. My new "opportunity lens" was, of course, just a temporary solution (it was a loan from my coach), and it was only applied to each specific "problem" as it presented itself.

On the other hand, as time went on and it continued to happen to me repeatedly throughout sessions, it eventually became into a habit. When anything upsetting happened, I would ask myself, "What might be good about this?" and "How can I use this?" before my coach would question me about it. and then have an open and pressure-free creative brainstorm about the several ways I might choose to react to the new circumstances.

My experience over the years has shown that it is beneficial for coaches and particularly leaders to make a habit out of asking yourself, "What's good about this?" in response to any circumstance that presents itself.

When I give seminars with leaders and managers who occasionally dispute this strategy as being an unrealistic sugar-coating of actual issues, I remind them of the words of British Field Marshall Bernard Montgomery, who was one of the harshest and most successful military commanders during World War II. I tell them that he was one of the toughest and most effective military leaders during World War II. He said that a leader should have an optimistic attitude that is contagious. The emotion you receive when you leave the presence of a leader after having a dialogue with them is the last measure of a leader's effectiveness. Do you have feelings of empowerment and self-assurance?

Too many of the leaders I've dealt with appear unconcerned with whether their followers leave a meeting feeling encouraged and inspired or downcast and disheartened. The human element is something that they do not take into account. They are, without even realizing it, undermining the creative energy, morale, and potential of the same individuals they are banking on to produce the products.

What The Trunk Of The Tree Is Supposed To Signify

Now the question is, what should our trunk be built of, and what should we leave out?

No matter what it is that we want to study, we must first have a firm grip of the fundamental ideas involved and the core of the material or the abilities that we want to acquire. The following is a list of some of the things that you need to concentrate on:

Fundamental ideas

Important foundations

Laws

Theories, as well as Fundamental Variations

Let's take a closer look at each one of them in more depth.

A. The fundamental ideas. By gaining a grasp of fundamental ideas, you are able to establish a foundation upon which you may build further knowledge throughout time. If you are unable to fully understand fundamental ideas, you will flood your brain, which will result in poor memory retention as well as learning that is either inefficient or shallow.

For example, the only way you'll be able to construct a robust understanding of economics is if you have a firm grasp of fundamental ideas such as supply and demand, inflation and deflation, monetary strategies, and the primary purpose of money. In addition to this, you will need to outline the essence of the economy in as much detail as possible. One such definition is as follows:

Economics is a field of study that focuses on finding efficient ways to distribute limited resources.

If there were an unlimited supply of resources, there would be no need for economics. Without having to make any concessions, we would just be able to acquire what we want whenever we want.

Consider the realm of politics as an alternative. If you want to have a more in-depth understanding of politics, it's probably a good idea to make sure that you can recognize the primary traits that set right-wing policies apart from left-wing ideas. It's possible that you don't agree with this differentiation or the two-party system that prevails in the majority of democracies. Despite this, it is a wonderful place to begin to get an understanding of politics. It provides you with a strong foundation upon which you may construct more information and hone your comprehension.

The important thing to remember is that it does not matter what you are studying; you must always focus on thoroughly comprehending the fundamental ideas behind whatever it is you are studying. Doing so will help you establish a strong foundation, which, in turn, will allow you to think more clearly and absorb more information throughout the course of your life.

Be Sincere In Your Concerns

It is imperative that you demonstrate real care for the people who are accountable to you as a leader if you want to achieve any level of success in this role. You can't make anything up to fool people about this. If you have trouble remembering information that is vital to the success of your staff, it is a good idea to write it down. If you know that someone's spouse had surgery the previous week, make it a point to inquire about how well they are recovering from the procedure. There is no need for you to become really precise. Simply mention, "How is Alice doing, I know you said she was going to be having a minor procedure?" Maintain an awareness of the things that are significant to them. If an employee informs you one day that he is going home to work on a broken lawn mower, you should ask him how things fared with the mower the next week. Has he gotten it straightened up yet? Was it a challenging task to do? Many of the individuals who work for you will have families, and their kids will likely take part in a variety of extracurricular activities. If they mention that they participated in a significant competition, don't forget to inquire about how things went for them there. Tell them that you hope they have a wonderful trip and that they make the most of their time off while they are getting ready for their holiday. Always inquire about how things turned out after they have returned. Where exactly have they gone? How was your time there? The more respect people have for you, the more interest they will take in what you have to say. Keep in mind that the ability to really and unselfishly care for other people is a sign of ethical maturity. Speaking in terms of the other person's interests is something that Dale Carnegie recommends doing in his book How to Win Friends and Influence People.

"When interacting with people, it is important to keep in mind that you are not dealing with logical creatures but rather emotional creatures." The works of Dale Carnegie

Do you want to damage your reputation with a member of the team? You won't get a response from me if you call, email, or text. Make it a goal to respond to each and every call. There are going to be instances when you are unable to. If I happen to miss a phone call, I make it a point to call the person back within fifteen minutes at the very latest. Spend the next half an hour on a text. One of these things is something that I like doing as well. I will send a text message to the person to let them know that I noticed where they called and that I will get back to them as soon as possible if I miss a phone call from them because I am too busy to call them back because of how busy I am. In other cases, I am able to deduce the reason why they phoned in the first place from the chat we had through text. Before you pick up the phone to give someone a second call, be sure you have a good reason for doing so. In preparation for our conversation, I prefer to take notes. Just so you know, the person on the other end of the phone can hear your beautiful grin. When you are speaking with your clients and your coworkers, smile. If at all possible, keep your phone calls to a minimum. The average workday includes a significant amount of unproductive time spent on the phone. You should make an effort to stand while you talk, and you should also move about or otherwise keep moving. It improves both your tone and your voice. Always remember to express your gratitude to the person who has taken your call or who has called you. As a leader, you should only text sometimes. It is possible for the words to be misunderstood, which would result in a great deal of trouble for you. You may use it either for the purpose I described above or to utter sentences that aren't too long. Never use it to submit material that is either too sensitive or too difficult to describe, since this might be seen as being overly ambiguous. Do not attempt to manage a team via the use of texting. I do make use of it sometimes while I am at a meeting, and I will elaborate more on that point in the next section. Pay undivided attention to the person with whom you are conversing. When you're on the phone, be sure to ask yourself this question. "What are they going through at this very moment?" Listen to what they have to say with real curiosity, and indicate that you care about what they have to say. Listen to the other person out before drawing any assumptions about them.

The Metaphor Of A Cake, As Well As A Rallying Cry For Future Leaders

If others believe you are unsure of yourself, they won't follow your lead. You truly want to be able to know for a fact that your objective is really ambitious, that you are capable of accomplishing it, and that the time is right for you to seize the chance. A vast number of individuals have aspirations of reaching the highest levels of their organizations, but they do not work toward achieving those goals and do not keep themselves prepared to do so.

If you keep waiting for the proper moment, the correct insight, or the ideal opportunity, it's possible that those things may never come your way, and the chance will pass you by. If you hadn't stopped them, others would have eaten your cake for them. In addition to going with what people seem to desire, one of our goals is to instill the confidence necessary to make the best choice.

A widespread problem in our society is that many people who are qualified but lack the self-assurance to speak out and distinguish themselves from the crowd. On the other hand, a large number of persons who are lacking in competence seem to have an abundance of confidence. Leaders are not those who do not experience fear or self-doubt; rather, they are those who experience the same fear and uncertainty that the rest of us do but choose to act in spite of those emotions.

Have you been giving up your slice of cake because you were unsure whether or not you should accept your share?

Be as intense as possible. Make sure you are. Maintain your clarity. That is very necessary.

142

WHAT IS IT THAT We Should Really Be Afraid Of?

The following quote from Marianne Williamson's book, Return to Love and a Gift of Change, covers all that needs to be said about the topic: "Our most fundamental fear isn't that we are inadequate.

Our deepest, darkest fear is that we are stronger than anybody could ever imagine. It is not our obscurity but rather our brightness that causes us the greatest concern. Our internal dialogue goes something like this: "Why should I be splendid, stunning, gifted, and marvelous?" In point of fact, who would you not be? ...When we shine our own light, we unintentionally make it possible for others to do the same. Because of the qualities that we exude, people are set free as we are liberated from our own fears.

That is a primary illustration of taking the initiative. People have no choice but to imitate those who carry themselves with self-assurance.

Rapport and Taking a Deep Breath

Pay close attention to the patterns of respiration shown by the individuals with whom you are engaging, specifically how they breathe. Should you take long or short breaths? How about a quick one? How does the rhythm of their breathing influence the pauses in their speech? The fundamental rhythm of the conversation may be seen to be reflected in the breathing patterns of the participants.

The following are some overarching interpretations that may be arrived at by observing the patterns of breathing used by a person. It is essential to keep in mind that the aforementioned guidelines are not applicable to every circumstance.

Reading an individual accurately might be more of a fluid process than following a precise guideline due to factors such as physical issues and poor habits. Because each person has their own unique method of communicating, it is impossible to generalize about how to properly read another person.

When someone is anxious or disturbed, their breathing may become shallower than normal.

Rapid breathing is a physical manifestation of emotions such as fear, excessive tension, or rage.

A rapid, deep breath or a sigh that is pushed out suggests that stress levels are rising.

A state of relaxation or focus is often indicated by slow, deep breaths.

After you have gotten a handle on someone's breathing pattern, you should gradually adjust your own breathing to make it similar to theirs and then go on as usual. Note the impact that this has on the interaction and keep it in mind moving forward. Mirroring (copying/mimicking) the breathing pattern of another person provides a number of useful advantages, one of which is the ability to guide someone into a new mental state when the technique is used well. Once you are in sync with someone's breathing rhythm, you will be able to gradually raise or decrease your own breathing pattern. The person with whom you are engaging will then follow your example and increase or decrease the pace at which they are breathing, which will cause them to either feel calmer or more energized.

Mirroring one's posture

Be wary of imitating someone else's posture; it is fairly simple to identify when it is done wrong. You will feel quite ridiculous if it is discovered that you have been mimicking the stance of another person. When you start paying closer attention to people's postures in general, you will realize that people are mimicking each other's postures all over the place.

It is not essential to mimic the motions and posture of another person exactly. The effect of mirroring may be accomplished with something as simple as the movement of one's hand. To get things off to a good start, try getting in the habit of taking a natural sip from your drink at the same time as the people you are with.

Develop Relationships With Your Staff Members.

Building relationships is an essential component of every manager's job responsibilities. It must be an ongoing and proactive conduct that is, or eventually becomes, the very core of any manager's personal style. This is a must.

Because it is going to be difficult for our employees to embrace the change that we are implementing, the connections that we have with them are going to be put under pressure as a result. It is nearly always our fault because we are doing something to them that is going to have an effect, and we are causing it.

When there has been little to no effort put forward to cultivate major connections with the people who make up a team, it will be far more difficult to

148

ensure that change is properly implemented.

This Is the Obstacle

It's not difficult to form new connections with people. It is challenging for many managers to carve out the appropriate amount of time to have meaningful talks with each and every member of their team. When this occurs, it is critical to take a careful look at the manner in which one spends their time and to examine other approaches to their job.

There are occasions when managers are not sufficiently concentrated to guarantee that they fulfill their responsibilities. It is far simpler to take on duties that require less effort, which results in less time being made available for the people they serve.

Building relationships is at the center of a manager's purview as an activity set. It is not the job to move a pen about or operate with items; rather, the job is to manage people. Any manager who is worthy of the title must make the welfare of their employees their first concern.

How to Carry It Out

One easy action that can be taken to improve the quality of your relationships is to make it a daily goal to have one-on-one conversations with a certain number of the individuals in your life. Make it a priority to ensure that the manner you communicate with them conveys respect for them.

One simple method for doing this is to encourage the other person to do the majority of the talking by asking open-ended questions that are designed to elicit information from them. When that is the objective, it will be simple for you to let them speak while you perform the majority of the listening.

This may have a tremendous impact that demonstrates to them that you care about them as people and that you are willing to take the time to make them feel like an important part of the team.